Plants
are alive!

by Molly Aloian

 Crabtree Publishing Company

www.crabtreebooks.com

Plants Close-Up

Author
Molly Aloian

Publishing plan research and development
Sean Charlebois, Reagan Miller
Crabtree Publishing Company

Editors
Reagan Miller, Kathy Middleton

Proofreader
Crystal Sikkens

Notes to adults
Reagan Miller

Photo research
Allison Napier, Ken Wright, Crystal Sikkens

Design
Ken Wright

Production coordinator and Prepress technician
Ken Wright

Print coordinator
Katherine Berti

Photographs
Wikimedia Commons: Kodak Z650: page 22
Other images by Shutterstock and Thinkstock

Library and Archives Canada Cataloguing in Publication

Aloian, Molly
   Plants are alive! / Molly Aloian.

(Plants close-up)
Includes index.
Issued also in electronic formats.
ISBN 978-0-7787-4219-7 (bound).--ISBN 978-0-7787-4224-1 (pbk.)

   1. Plants--Juvenile literature. 2. Plant anatomy--Juvenile
literature. 3. Plant life cycles--Juvenile literature. I. Title.
II. Series: Plants close-up

QK49.A46 2012   j580   C2012-900407-3

Library of Congress Cataloging-in-Publication Data

Aloian, Molly.
 Plants are alive! / Molly Aloian.
    p. cm. -- (Plants close-up)
 Includes index.
  ISBN 978-0-7787-4219-7 (reinforced library binding : alk. paper) --
 ISBN 978-0-7787-4224-1 (pbk. : alk. paper) -- ISBN 978-1-4271-7904-3
 (electronic pdf) -- ISBN 978-1-4271-8019-3 (electronic html)
 1. Plants--Juvenile literature. 2. Plants--Life cycles--Juvenile literature.
 I. Title.

 QK49.A456 2012
 580--dc23
                                        2012001127

Crabtree Publishing Company
www.crabtreebooks.com   1-800-387-7650

Printed in Canada/042012/KR20120316

Published in Canada
Crabtree Publishing
616 Welland Ave.
St. Catharines, Ontario
L2M 5V6

Published in the United States
Crabtree Publishing
PMB 59051
350 Fifth Avenue, 59th Floor
New York, New York 10118

Published in the United Kingdom
Crabtree Publishing
Maritime House
Basin Road North, Hove
BN41 1WR

Published in Australia
Crabtree Publishing
3 Charles Street
Coburg North
VIC 3058

Contents

Living things

There are hundreds of thousands of different kinds of plants on Earth. All plants are alive. Plants are living things.

Like all living things, plants need food to grow and stay alive. They make their own food from air, sunlight, water, and nutrients.

Plant parts

leaves

stem

roots

All plants have **roots**, **stems**, and **leaves**. Some plants also have **flowers**.

A flower is the part of a plant that makes **seeds**. Some plants make many seeds. Other plants make just one seed.

The roots

A plant's roots grow under the ground and help hold the plant in the soil. Roots take in water and nutrients from soil.

The roots also store food for the plant.

The stem

A plant's stem helps hold the plant upright.

The stem holds the leaves upright, too.

The stem carries water and nutrients from the roots to the leaves and flowers.

The leaves

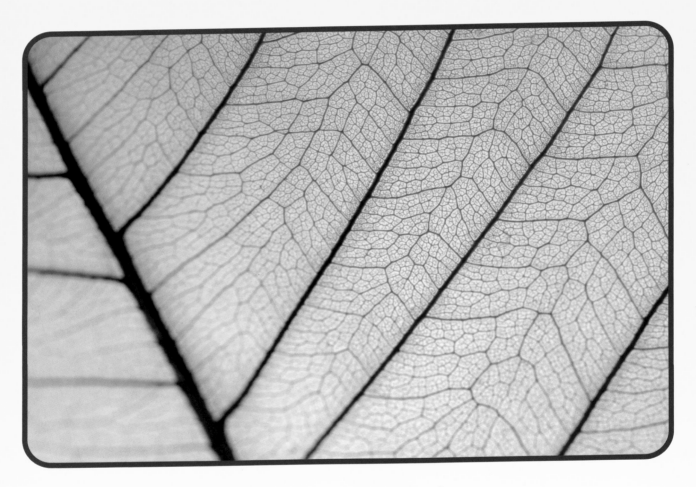

A plant's leaves take in sunlight.

The plant uses sunlight to make food.

Some plants have big leaves.

Other plants have small leaves.

Flowers

Many plants have flowers. Flowers are the parts of the plant that make seeds.

Petals are the colorful leaves of a flower.

A plant's life cycle

The flower on a fully grown plant can make seeds. New plants grow from seeds.

The seeds of some plants drop down into the soil below. Other seeds are blown off of flowers and carried by the wind to soil in other places.

Sprout to seedling

When a seed starts to grow in soil, it sprouts.
First, the seed coat covering the seed breaks
open. Then a tiny root grows down into the soil.

Next, a shoot grows upward toward sunlight.

It grows into a young plant called a **seedling**.

Making Seeds

flower bud

As a seedling grows, it forms leaf and flower buds. A flower bud is a flower that has not yet opened.

pollen

The flower will open when the plant is ready to make seeds. Most plants need a powder called pollen from other flowers to make seeds.

Friendly helpers

Bees and other insects carry pollen from flower to flower. Then the plant can make its own seeds.

The plant's seeds will become new plants, and a new **life cycle** begins.

Words to know

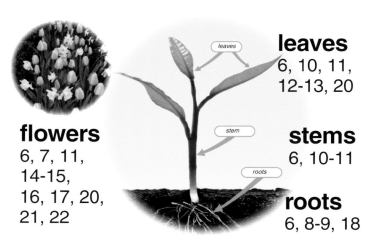

leaves

stem

roots

flowers
6, 7, 11,
14-15,
16, 17, 20,
21, 22

leaves
6, 10, 11,
12-13, 20

stems
6, 10-11

roots
6, 8-9, 18

life cycle 16-23

seedling
18-19, 20

seeds
7, 14, 16-18, 20-23

Notes for adults and an experiment

What do plants need?

• Instructions to adult: Provide each child with three clear cups, soil, and three beans. Have them plant each bean in a cup about one inch (2.5 cm) deep in soil. Children will label the plants:

    Plant 1: Sunlight and Water
    Plant 2: Sunlight only
    Plant 3: Water only

Put Plant 3 in a dark closet or inside a can with a dark lid. Place the other two plants in a sunny window. Remind children to water Plants 1 and 3 when the soil feels dry. Plant 2 gets no water. Next, encourage children to predict what will happen. Ask them which plant they think will grow first and why?

• Recording observations: Children can record their observations (e.g. plant height) in a plant journal every day. After 7-10 days, invite children to share their conclusions about what plants need to grow.

Learn more

Books

Plants are living things (Introducing Living Things) by Bobbie Kalman. Crabtree Publishing Company (2007)

A Bean s Life (Crabtree Connections) by Angela Royston. Crabtree Publishing Company (2011)

Websites

The Great Plant Escape : Children team up with Detective LePlant to identify plant parts and functions and explore how a plant grows.
http://urbanext.illinois.edu/gpe/index.cfm

Michigan 4-H Children's Garden Tour: This interactive site takes visitors on a virtual garden tour. Children learn about different kinds of plants, play educational games, and answer questions.
http://4hgarden.msu.edu/kidstour/tour.html